T0121089

Whispers of Hope

Lessons Learned from a Trauma Survivor

GEORGIANA WHITE

WESTBOW
P R E S S®
A DIVISION OF THOMAS NELSON
& ZONDERVAN

WestBow Press books may be ordered through booksellers or by contacting:

WestBow Press
A Division of Thomas Nelson & Zondervan
1663 Liberty Drive
Bloomington, IN 47403
www.westbowpress.com
844-714-3454

ISBN: 978-1-6642-4232-6 (sc)
ISBN: 978-1-6642-4233-3 (e)

Library of Congress Control Number: 2021915986

Print information available on the last page.

WestBow Press rev. date: 08/23/2021

To all the survivors, the misfits, or the unloved,

This book is for you.

Contents

Preface ix

Acknowledgments xi

Introduction xiii

The Girl Next Door 1

You Matter, Your Voice Matters 5

Just Breathe: You Will Get Through This 11

You Are Worthy, You Are Valuable, You Are
Important 17

You Can Always Begin Again, This Time For You.... 23

Compassion Is Not A Virtue; It's A Commitment...... 27

Conclusion 31

Afterword 37

Preface

All too often in life we try to rationalize why bad things happen to good people. My fascination with karmic justice started when I was in elementary school. Having grown up in a deeply religious community, we were raised that anything good or bad was done by the will of God. This would send me on a lifelong quest to understand and know God. What I learned is that God, like gravity, is often felt but rarely seen. I believe God can often be witnessed in the hidden angels you don't realize have touched your life until long after they have gone.

When I truly began my search for God, I knew I needed to analyze and unpack years of trauma and neuroses to be able to understand why things happened the way they did. I wanted to leave behind all the grudges and hurt feelings so that I could live a more positive life. This led me on a journey of self-healing and positive living. To write this book I had to relive each experience and evaluate my part in each situation. Because that's the thing; just as much as I had been hurt, I had to admit I had a part to play. There was some takeaway that I had to learn. I figured I would share my experiences and lessons learned to help someone who might be going through something similar so that they know they are not alone. Hope you enjoy!

Acknowledgments

There are so many people who helped contribute to the making of this book. To thank them would be to thank everyone who helped me survive. I especially want to thank my soul tribe. You all have kept me going through everything. My partner in crime, I know I would not be here without you. Thank you for always showing me what I aspire to be. And to my muse, words cannot describe what you have given me. Thank you for restoring my faith in humanity and showing me there are good people in the world. I love you. This is just the beginning!

Introduction

I guess in the end, you start to look back at the beginning. I think back to running around in the sun under rainbows of water from the garden hose. Laughing and horseplaying, oblivious to the realities of the world. Even as a child, curiosity and a need to have order led me to ask the really tough questions. First, to question my fourth-grade catechism teacher about the logic behind Catholic doctrine. Then later to question my place and purpose on this earth. Needless to say, with a thirst for knowledge and a no-back-down attitude, I have been in a scrape or two. I should start by saying I am not a self-help guru or a spiritual leader. I am just a girl who happens to have had a lot of stuff happen to her. I do not have a degree in psychology; nor am I a licensed therapist. What I am an expert in is survival. What I offer is a story of hope and resilience of the human spirit.

After spending a ridiculous amount of time watching survival shows, I have picked up a thing or two. I wanted to know that in any situation I would always be able to be safe. I guess that's why I clung to religion so much. I yearned for the safety and security of God's love and never-exhausted forgiveness. I spent a long time living in this mode. It was only when I tried to be a better person that I was provided with the lessons I would have to learn to truly be happy and come from a place of compassion and love. That led me to research what it really meant to be happy and whether God truly exists.

Then I went down the rabbit hole of physics.—from transference of energy laws to the laws of the universe and the power of positivity. The following lessons are the result of the analyzation for your exploration.

The Girl Next Door

A llow me to start at the beginning. I was born to working-class parents. We lived in a lower-middle-class neighborhood. Back then it was safe to walk by yourself around the neighborhood. In those times, people took care of each other, even if they were strangers. My father was a welder, and my mother was a teacher. I was the only sister to two older brothers, Greg and Quincy. My oldest brother, Quincy, couldn't care less whether I was around or not. The eight-year age gap keeping us from bonding. I think he literally blocked my existence out for a whole year, preferring to read comic books. My youngest brother, Greg, on the other hand, was my henchman from a young age. My parents, being traditional, forbid me from going anywhere without a chaperone, which of course left me with an uncontrollable urge to disobey authority and be a maverick whenever possible.

Which is probably why my mother strongly pushed me into singing in the church choir. Every facet of life in my house was based around our faith. As a young and naïve girl, I thought everything in life, both good and bad, was the direct result of God's wrath or favor. A fact that would lead me toward a push/pull relationship with faith.

I was groomed from a young age to be a wife and mother. At least that is what my parents always wanted, and I was influenced to want the same things. The problem was my dreams always reached higher than that.

My mother was born to a retired railroad worker and a homemaker. She lived with nothing but constant responsibilities. My grandparents were extremely traditional. They still believed children were meant to be seen and not heard. And they adopted a "spare the rod spoil the child" mentality. Even as a child, I was always independent and driven. If anyone said I could not do something, it became my sole mission to prove that person wrong. This would prove to get me through some of the darkest times of my life.

My father, in contrast to my mother, was the youngest of two and, therefore, the baby. And he was treated as such. Oddly enough, my parents complemented each other in a codependent and dysfunctional way. He was strong-willed and brass, and my mother was docile and accommodating. That is not to say she was weak. To have lived through thirty years tied to a man like my father, you would have to have backbone.

Things were simpler then. I had no need to look at any other avenues of achievement. Good grades and behavior were expected, but academic success was not. If the good grades came in on my report card, and if no one from the school called my parents, I could fly under the radar. It was not that they did not care about me. It was just that by the time I came along, they had their hands full. Unfortunately, this left me with a compulsive need to seek their affection through approval as a person and the things I did. Every action I took revolved around avoiding the displeasure of others.

> *Takeaway:* As parents, we want our kids to be more in life than we were. Unfortunately, this has the side effect of training our kids to be what we want them to be instead of who they naturally are.

As a kid, I always felt like I had to get good grades to make my parents proud. I never felt like I was enough just the way I was. What I have come to realize is that each person is special in his or her own way. As they say, God does not make mistakes. Bad habits or traits are often learned and can lead us astray. And if bad things are learned, good things can replace the bad.

I say, foster the innocence of children if possible. The argument has also been made that keeping reality from children leads to children unable to deal with life once they leave the nest. I have experienced that life is going to happen to you whether you look for it or not. So why not enjoy the ignorant bliss that childhood brings? Why rob kids of that chance?

Family expectations can take you down a dangerous path. Not only to your self-esteem but also to your identity of self. Trying to make your family happy will have you turning yourself inside out to be someone you are not. As a result, you must then go back and retrain yourself to unlearn the toxic behaviors you were taught. I can tell you that this is an exhausting and confusing journey. Whenever possible, stay true to who you are and what you genuinely want. After all, we are all given this one life. Make it yours.

You Matter, Your Voice Matters

Trying to remember my childhood is similar to putting together a puzzle all the while knowing the pieces aren't all there. What was prevalent was an innocent optimism for dreams of the fairy-tale life waiting to manifest.

When doing research on healing from childhood trauma, I learned one of the response mechanisms is to try constantly to please everyone else. There is fear that if you don't, they will reject you. Growing up, I remember wanting to sink into the background whether it was to avoid punishment or rejection. Generally it was not a good thing to be noticed. Being a people-pleaser as a child, I always tried to go out of my way to gain the approval of the adults around me. Unfortunately, at the age of eleven, I was abused by a family friend.

So many trauma survivors describe an out-of-body experience during the attack. I vividly recall the sensation of being frozen inside my own body and head. I was unable to believe what was happening. It was as if I was outside myself, watching the situation play out on a television set. It was like some bad movie where you yell at the main character and shout all the things you would do if you were in the situation. I felt so ugly and ashamed.

I remember curling into a ball and the feeling of the cold tiles against my face as my tears drenched my cheeks. My cheeks stuck to the floor with the moisture. I couldn't make sense of what had just happened. I trusted this person. How could they do this to me. Why? They had always been my ally and confidant. They made me feel seen and special in a world where I would often go unnoticed. I knew the person loved me, so how could I wrap my head around what they were capable of. I had no time to figure this out or dwell on it. The way I saw it I could tell my parents or pretend like it never happened. Thinking of the spanking I would likely endure for "lying" on the person, telling my parents was out of the question. Also, I didn't want the person to get into trouble. It would be okay. I could cry, and everything would go away. But it did not go away. I said nothing. Nor did he and the abuse continued for six years. I'm not sure what I expected him to say. I suppose I looked to him for guidance. The fact that it was never talked about or even mentioned could have contributed to the normalization of abuse. As if it wasn't even worth discussing. Only later would I discover that this was indeed "Grooming." It was a very strategic form of abuse. So covert that victims often don't know that they had been indoctrinated into secrecy.

However, not understanding this at the time would lead to a huge buildup of resentment. I resented my parents for not paying attention and looking deeper to see the truth. How could they not notice? How could they not see me wearing clothes three sizes too big? How could they not see me turn away in disgust anytime I had to hug that family friend goodbye or hello? How could they not pay attention to the extreme measures I took to avoid being alone with him? How could they *not* see? They were my parents. Through the eyes of innocence, I always assumed my mother knew me best of all. I thought that if they knew me so well, they would be able to know intuitively something was wrong and save me. I understand how simple that line of thinking is. The truth is probably more complex.

As a result of the abuse, when faced with uncomfortable situations, particularly dealing with older men, I would climb inside myself. I would close my eyes and try to go somewhere else mentally. And for years, no one knew a thing. I never let on to anyone that something was not right. I just endured.[1] Recent studies of trauma indicate

---

[1] Frey, Rebecca J. "Dissociation and Dissociative Disorders." *Encyclopedia of Mental Disorders*, www.minddisorders.com/Del-Fi/Dissociation-and-dissociative-disorders.html#:~:text=Recent%20studies%20of%20trauma%20indicate%20that%20the%20human,affected%20person%20cannot%20control%20or%20%22edit%22%20these%20memories.

that the human brain stores traumatic memories in a different way than normal memories are stored. Traumatic memories are not processed. They are integrated into a person's ongoing life in the same fashion as normal memories. Patients who have the compartmentalized type of dissociation do not engage in conscious integration or mental systems, and do not or cannot consciously access certain areas of memory or information that would normally be available.

It wasn't until I sought therapy for childhood trauma that I began to unravel the years of compartmentalized memories. For the first time I began to talk openly about what I experienced. Even though I was a child, I resented myself for not stopping it from happening. And saddest of all, I thought that even if I did tell people, no one would believe me. I buried my secret in the darkest recesses of my mind. It was only after watching Groomed, an 2021 American documentary film, directed and produced by Gwen van de Pas that I realized that this is precisely what I had experienced as a child. This helped me to see the abuse in a different light. No longer was I the magnet for abuse, I was at the time easy prey.

For the longest time, I did not talk about it. I suffered for fear that no one would believe me—or worse, that I would be blamed. But that is just it; I was not. That is the thing they never tell you about abuse. Often the abuser manages to convince you it was your fault. That somehow you had deserved the abuse. That is how abusers can get away with it and move on to abuse other people.

We must stop keeping quiet. I know what I am asking. I know and have felt how difficult it can be to come forward with your truth. I have lost a lot of family because of speaking my truth. But the trade-off is freedom. I finally stopped feeling dirty and ashamed. I finally felt like I could start to build my strength back up. That is the issue though. It was not something I should have taken on in the first place. It was not my shame or embarrassment. It was *his* shame and embarrassment. So if you are in an unsafe situation—mentally, physically, or sexually—please say something. And remember, people do care. And you are loved.[2]

Trying to communicate about the abuse to someone who has never been through the same trauma is often more isolating than the retelling. This was my case. When trying to explain my thoughts, defense, coping mechanisms, and triggers often left me feeling isolated and alone. Like no one understood what I was feeling. People can sympathize and empathize, but they will never grasp it. For generations, the established patriarchy has enabled continued victimization because as a generation, we are taught not to air our dirty laundry. Adopting the "What happens in the family stays in the family" mentality. Hordes of family lineages have been altered because of

---

[2] The following are available to help if you have been subject to rape and other forms of violence: The Rape Crisis 24 Hour Hotline, 210-349-7273, https://rapecrisis.com; National Domestic Violence Hotline, 1-800-799-7233, https://Quincy.thehotline.org; National Suicide Prevention 24-Hour Lifeline, 1-800-273-8255, https://suicidepreventionlifeline.org.

this indoctrination. This took me a lifetime to wrap my head around. It was never about me. It was about the feeling of gratification my abuser obtained resulting from the attack. Where there is one there are generally more. Predators target certain individuals based on a number of factors, chiefly ease of access and susceptibility. This means they can get close and gain your trust to exploit the situation. It in no way is indicative of you wanting an assault to happen or that you were, "asking for it." No one asks to be violated.

Just Breathe: You Will Get Through This

You know how you hear about random people getting struck by lightning, but you never think it's going to happen to you? That was what it was like when my mom got sick. I had a dentist appointment the day the bomb dropped. This typically meant I would go to work with my mom and miss school for the day. The first indication anything was wrong was when she started to sob, and her coworkers stood with their arms around her, consoling her. At the age of thirteen, I hadn't understood what was happening. Until then I did not know much about sickness or what was going on around me. From one day to the next, it seemed her stomach became swollen until she looked to be in her third trimester. My parents hid all this from me, of course. They would say they were going to run an errand, and I could not come because it was just going to be in and out. They would go to the hospital a couple times a week to flush out the accumulated water in her stomach. Doctors could not figure out why, so they performed a bunch of tests and tried a bunch of medicine, basically throwing darts in the dark and see which one stuck. Finally, after many sick days and "errands" run, doctors identified a cyst on her ovary. To my young mind I thought, *Oh, problem solved. They will take it out, and life will go on just as before.*" Doctors had concluded that a hysterectomy was necessary to take out the cancerous cyst and hopefully remove all remnants of the cancer.

The day of her operation, I remember walking into her hospital room. She was sitting on the only visitor's chair in the room with a hospital gown on. She tried to hide the fact that she had been crying, but her red nose and misty eyes betrayed her. She admitted she was crying because she feared that she was not going to be a woman anymore. For a woman not to be able to bear children, it can make you feel like the greatest failure. In our culture, a woman's main job on this earth was to have children and be a wife to your husband. I think it made her question her womanhood or what made her a woman. I told her in a whisper, "Mom, it's okay. It's fine. Besides, how can you get better after me," comically stated with an exaggerated bow. This calmed her down enough for her to give me a small smile.

Prior to being wheeled out to go to the operating room, she gave each of us a hug. To Quincy she said, "Take care of them." To Greg she said, "Keep yourself out of trouble." Finally she turned to me and said, "Do good in school, and do your homework." For me it was just as it should be. I was saying goodbye, and I would see her the next day. I had no idea what was to come. She was in ICU in recovery, and overnight, it seemed she got worse every day. I could see the distress in her face. She looked so very tired, as if she fighting a one-woman battle and losing.

The light in the darkness was the first thing I remember. My dad crying and frantic, demanding I get up and saying we had to get to the hospital before it was too late. *Too late for what?* I wondered. *Visiting hours? Why was there such an urgency to get there?* And this being the night of my brothers' military ball, they were not home to ride with us. I was so confused, but I did not know what to be confused about. In my young mind, she was just going to be there for a little bit to get treated, and then she was going to come home. Everything would be fine. My dad knew the truth, but he could never bring himself to tell me. He never explained it to me, no one did. I guess they thought they were protecting me. Possibly they thought, *Oh, she's a kid. She doesn't need to know about this.* Nobody told me my entire world was about to be broken.

Dad sped the whole way to the hospital, running through traffic lights with his hazard lights on. I warned him to stop doing that. If cops caught him, they would give him a ticket, and it would take even longer. He explained that if you have your hazard lights on, they will follow you to the hospital, but they will not pull you over. Which to this day I still do not even know if that is true.

But we were already too late.

Walking into the recovery room, I spotted my mom free of all the tubes and machines she had accumulated during her stay. She looked like she was sleeping. It was just my mom again, beautiful and peaceful. But she was not asleep. Her skin was cold to the touch and lifeless. In that moment I begged God to bring her back. I swore eternal fidelity and service if he would just bring her back. He had allowed Jesus to perform miracles; he could do it again. Especially for one of his most faithful followers. She prayed the rosary every day going and leaving work. God would not punish her or us like this. This was not happening. It just could not be happening. God would not do this. Whatever I had done wrong, punish me but leave her here. I was not done being raised; there was still so much I did not know. How was I supposed to do this? My orbit revolved around her being my sun, and she was gone. I begged my mom to come back. There must be a little bit of her still in there, and if there were, she was going to fight her way back to us. She just could not be gone, I begged God once more: "Bring her back, please. Please. Please. I'm not ready to do this without her." But he never did. No matter how hard I focused on her, there was no indication of survival.

For the next few days I was on autopilot. I just sat there watching everything happening around me—having no feeling, having no concept of reality—just watching the world go by. People called to ask if they could help. People asked if they could bring by casseroles and to offer their condolences. People said if we ever needed anything just to call. But to a thirteen-year-old girl mad at the world and everything in it, nothing anyone did or said would make it better; it was only making it worse. People would say, "She's in a better place now. She is resting now. Everything heals with time. Everything happens for a reason." In hindsight, I see the efforts in their consolation, but in my young selfish mind, all I wanted was my mom back. I knew time was moving on, but I just could not feel it, hear it, or see it.

The day of her funeral, I shook hands after hands until there was only a couple of people left, and then it was time. The moment I had been avoiding the entire day had come, and I had to face the reality that my hero was gone and was not coming back. The moment that they closed her casket I did not want to let her go. I knew that I could not; she would not want me to. Being the woman that she was, she would have immediately risen out of her casket to tell me to get up. I could almost hear her directing me not to quit! She would say, "You're not a quitter! Get up and keep fighting! I do not care how much it hurts. I do not care how much you want to give up. I do not care what happened to you or what you did wrong. You do not stop till you are dead and buried. And even then, give God what for! You are your mother's daughter!" So I pressed my hand against the pew and slowly but surely, I rose.

Takeaway: If there is one thing I can assure you, in life you will go through tough times. I am not talking about the everyday stresses of bills and responsibilities. I am talking about the times that will define who you are. The times that have you feeling out of control and desperate. Unfortunately, I know this feeling well. I cannot tell you anything that will take it away and make it better. What I can tell you is that in life there tends to be ebbs and flows. Just as the bad times come, the good times will follow. Nothing lasts forever, the good or the bad. I know it can be hard to keep going when you have no ambition to, but just breathe. If you can make it through one minute, you can make it through the next. And if you can make it five minutes, you can make it ten. If you can make it an hour, the next hour is achievable. That is the key to survival. It is not just getting up again and never giving up. That is what you do when you get knocked down. When you are broken, though, the only thing I have found to get me through is to try not to focus on the big picture and just take things a minute at a time. Eventually you will climb your way out, one inch at a time. Just don't stop moving forward.

You Are Worthy, You Are Valuable, You Are Important

"A narcissist, by definition, is someone with a pervasive pattern of grandiosity, need for admiration, and lack of empathy, whose symptoms begin in early adulthood,"[3] says Cory Newman, PhD, a professor of psychology at the Perelman School of Medicine at the University of Pennsylvania. A narcissist is described as a self-absorbed person, especially when it comes to relationships of all kinds—romantic, familial, workplace, even friendships. A person who put his or her needs and desires above those of another person. What they do not tell you is that they are typically charming

---

[3] McGilvary, Reuben. "The Dark Side of Narcissism." *Reuben McGilvary.com*, July 7, 2019, Quincy.reubenmcgilvary.com/post/the-dark-side-of-narcissism.

and often say exactly the right things They also subtly plant insecurities in you until you live entirely for their approval, often losing your own personality. This is exactly what happened to me.

It's wondrous how a person can completely go against one's beliefs to obtain the approval of a narcissist. And unfortunately, all too often great people end up not only questioning what is wrong with them but blaming themselves for the behaviors of others. It's amazing how stealth the process is.

The details of the relationship don't matter as much as the lesson. I spent so much time invested in "our" happiness. I was devoid of any idea who I was. All I wanted was for him to love me, but no matter what I said or did, it was out of my control. It was probably one of the most difficult times of my life. I remember sitting on a friend's couch crying, asking her, "What did I do? Why me? What can I have possibly done that was so bad that he would feel like it's okay to treat me like I wasn't even human? What can I have done differently?" She helped me to understand that when it comes to that situation, sometimes there is nothing you can do. He was going to do what he wanted to do because he wanted to do it, and he would find a justification whether one existed or not. He would not take responsibility or be accountable for the things that he did. It took me a long time to learn that this In no way was that a reflection of me as a woman or my value as a person. Additionally, anyone who has had experience with a narcissistic person can testify that they will never admit wrongdoing, they are incapable. This in no way devalues a victim's experience or trauma suffered through the experience.

Unfortunately, my parents, although they did teach me how to be a wife and a mother, did not teach me how to value myself. They did not teach me that for someone to be with me was a gift to that person, not a gift to me. As human beings we all inherently have value. And as cliché as it is, all individuals have value as creations of God and the universe. It's a surreal and humbling thought. I think that had my parents taught me and instilled in me my value as a human being, I would have seen red flags earlier. I would have demanded my worth. There are 7.9 billion people in this world. Somebody was going to love and value me the way that I deserved. This is something that, with the help of my support system, I had to teach myself. But how does one even begin to love themselves? I thought I always had a healthy opinion of myself, self esteem is a whole different monster entirely. This is what keeps people in toxic and unhealthy situations. For a variety of reasons, in my experience stemming from negative self talk, people often feel like they are undeserving of better. They can only see the drawbacks to their character, appearance, or social and financial standing. They can't see the wonderful and valuable person that encompasses so much more that just that. Those are details of where a person is in that time of life.

Takeaway: I do not care what anyone else says, you are a king or a queen. King Hollis is an excellent motivational speaker, and he can explain this better than I can, so I will reference his YouTube videos. By virtue of having been born on this earth, we inherently have value. Over time and after certain interactions, we lose sight of that. I am here to remind you, you are valuable. There is only one you in this world, and that is what makes you special. Even if you say, "Well, I didn't do anything with my life. I messed up. I am too this or that." To that I say, "So what?" If there is breath in your lungs and a beat to your heart, you can start again. You deserve the best in life. Everyone deserves to feel loved and respected because everyone is human. As human beings, we need to start to appreciate and empathize with each other. We must start building each other up because you never know the effect you can have on a person if you take time to try. What else are we put on this earth for if not to make it a better place?

But you cannot pour from an empty cup. It is impossible to show unconditional love to another human being unless you have self-love. Trying to leads to compromising your value and worth to bring someone else up. Recognize your importance and individuality, and never let anyone make you feel less than.

You Can Always Begin Again,
This Time For You

Sophomore year in college, I saw a video called, *The Human Experience*. When referencing the Peruvian orphanage experience, what struck me was the positivity and resilience shown by the kids. To see how these kids in such horrible conditions can still have such joy and light was awe-inspiring. I had been thinking about everything that had gone on in my life, and I realized I was playing the victim. I was only thinking, *Why me? Why is this happening to me? I do not deserve it; I am a good person. Why did I go through all that?*

So I decided at that moment to hit reset. I quit school, I isolated myself from anyone who was a negative influence, and decided to take a good, hard look at myself. What was going to make me happy? Regardless of what was going on with anyone else, I just hit reset. I decided from that day forward to do only what was in my best interest and what was going to make me happy. I was not going to live for anyone else anymore.

I was going to live true to myself, and I was never going to lose myself again. I took some time off to get my head right. I decided what I wanted, and what I would have to do to get me there. Most of all, I had to congratulate myself and give myself a break. Regardless of how far I got from there, I made it through everything that was meant to break me. I restarted life with a new perspective.

I have been extremely blessed with an amazing support system. To have that support structure was really an amazing experience and influential in getting through everything. Eventually I made it through school, and I graduated. The only reason I was able to graduate was because I refused to quit. One step at a time I did it. Oddly enough, this is also when I started to be able to spot God's hand through people.

> *Takeaway:* Learn to forgive yourself and try again. It can be incredibly hard to forgive yourself, especially when your error severely affected your life. All I can say is you do not know what you do not know. If one does not know how to wash his or her hands, should that individual's hands stay dirty? Should that person feel

guilty about it? In the same way, we are often not given the tools to navigate life successfully in a positive, constructive way. We must learn the hard way. And that is okay. It is okay to fail. Failing one time is okay; letting it keep you there is not. Every failure has a lesson in it. If you tried something and it did not go the way you wanted it to, that is okay because you gained valuable knowledge of what *not* to do. Then you can try again and do something different. By process of elimination, the right answer will come. It might not come easily, and you will more than likely have to work for it. But think about how amazing it will feel when you finally succeed. That standing at the mountaintop feeling is unbeatable. It does not matter how tall the mountain is; do not look up or down. Just take it an inch at a time, and before you know it, you will get there. Don't stop; stay true on the way up. Often it is not reaching the top that defines you. It's what you did to get there.

Compassion Is Not A Virtue;
It's A Commitment

Whether good or bad, my father was always a strong person. Strong of will and especially a strong of personality. So when he started getting sick, I had no reason to think that would change. My dad had been chronically sick for a while, mostly back and leg pains. One day I came home from school, and he was having trouble breathing. I took him to the hospital to make sure he was okay. After doctors looked him over, they decided to admit him because apparently he was having a stroke. Just like that. He did not show any of the normal signs associated with a stroke, but they rushed him into the emergency room. After testing was completed, he was diagnosed with end stage cirrhosis.

I, of course, had no idea what that meant. The doctor explained there was no treatment at this stage, and the damage due to lack of oxygen had left him needing care for his remaining days. To my naïve mind, this was just another illness that he would take medication for. When the social worker from the hospital recommended he be put on hospice care, I just assumed it would be the same as having a home health-care provider. Someone would come to his house to cook and clean for him. No big deal. How wrong I was.

Overnight it seemed his health deteriorated at a fast rate. One day he was walking around and joking, albeit with difficulty, and the next he could not do anything for himself. He had become a shell of the man I once knew.

The truth was my dad was dying. He was never going to get better and would only get worse. He would become frustrated with himself and his new disabilities. My father, once a proud and boastful man, was now diminished to a stumbling old man barely able to make it to the bathroom in time.

The nurses eventually informed us that he was most definitely not going to get any better. The last night I saw my dad alive, he woke me up from a dead sleep in the morning in a panic. He gasped, unable to catch his breath, and was rushed to the hospital. Doctors thought the best course of action was to induce a coma to allow his body a chance to repair itself. Again the situation was experienced through a television screen. I knew everything was happening and that I held the responsibility for what came next. It was in my hands to decide the man's fate. Lord how I did not want the responsibility. The uncertainty of the situation is indescribable. You hear so many unlikely stories of miracles happening and people coming out of a coma to live an abundant life. I knew after all the information obtained until this point that to continue to keep my father on life support was to prolong his suffering. Flashes of him weeping at his diminished state flashed before my eyes. I thought of how vibrant and jovial he was as opposed to the person lying before me in the hospital bed. The decision although crushing was as I saw it an act of mercy.

When the time came, I spoke to the doctors at the hospital and asked if he was ever going to come back, even if only by a small possibility. They responded with a resounding no. No matter what kind of man he was, he was still my father. In a voice barely above a whisper, I told the doctors to unplug the machine. And I immediately broke down. Even though it was the right thing to do, for years I would wonder if it was the right decision. I had to let the only parent I had left go.

> *Takeaway:* The hardest thing in life is to show compassion to someone who has profoundly wronged you. Even if it is not family, to truly be a good person, there will come a time when you must forgive someone who is not sorry. Forgiveness does not mean acceptance. You can

forgive someone and want nothing to do with that individual. Forgiveness is just acknowledging there was a wrong done and the fact that you will no longer let it have a negative effect on you. No one deserves that much power over you. Anger is like a disease. It seeps into who you are and turns your heart cold to the suffering of others. Do not get me wrong; it is a lot easier. To have anger and to hate is to shut off humanity and the ability to feel emotions like hurt and disappointment. It is a Band-Aid, and it must be ripped off eventually. There are many things in life that can make you want to go down that road. Long term, the effects just are not worth it. People you love will start to distance themselves to protect themselves. The quality of the people you do have around you will go down as misery loves company. And as was the case with my father, at the end of your life, all the damage you did during your life determines what your end looks like. So it is just a decision of what you want that to look like.

Conclusion

After all that has happened to me, I think the takeaway is this. and this is perhaps the hardest truth to learn: People will leave you whether willingly or unwillingly. People will hurt you and disappoint you. The only surety you have in life is that no matter the situation you find yourself in, the constant is you. You may not be able to control the situation or the circumstances, but what you can decide is how you will handle it. You can choose to see the hope in a bad situation, or you can focus on the injustice and unfairness of it all. That's the funny thing about hope. I always thought having hope was being endlessly optimistic and refusing to de dragged down by the ugly reality. I have since learned that hope is having faith that it will be ok. It's not knowing how or when the dark night of the soul will end, it is just knowing it will. If you decide to be positive and make lemonade out of lemons, no matter how bitter, the lemonade will still have some sweetness. And the better you get at it, the sweeter and more abundant the flavor.

Things will happen in your life that will change you. It will either change the way you think or change your entire view on issues. Let it. Do not be afraid to change just because it is new or never been done. Change is evolution in process. And at the end of everything, you might find you end up being the person you were always meant to be if life and people had not thrown you off course. In society today, we are engrained with a need to obtain the approval of the people around us. This also comes with the need to fulfill the expectations of others. This can create a feeling of accomplishment or failure based on the opinion of those around you. That's the thing. It is just that the opinion of others. We all have one life to do with as we see fit and attempting to live for someone else can lead someone down a very dark path.

Les Brown, one of the best motivational speakers, puts it this way: "When life knocks you down, try to land on your back. Because if you can look up, you can get up." And it is emphatically true. Life will knock you down; it will knock the wind out of you. And it will most definitely test your resolve to get back up. But if you can look up and know that you are still alive, you have everything you need to make the biggest comeback this world has ever seen. That is not to say it will be easy or fast. You want easy or fast, go through the drive-through at McDonalds. Do not try to go through at lunchtime, though, because you will be waiting. It will take hard work; it will take sacrifice and tears. And just when you think you are beaten down and have nothing left to give, catch your breath and try again. Failure doesn't mean you have lost. Failure is always figuring out what did not work so that you know what angle to try next. And through the process of elimination, one angle will work. It may not be the most comfortable, and it most definitely will cause you to step out of your comfort zone. But do it anyway.

Every great accomplishment started with an idea that turned into a dream. Ordinary men and women who refused to cower to society and what they were told was possible and acceptable. And like me, you may be thinking, *I cannot do that. I do not have the time, money, or commitment to go through with something so huge.* And while you may not, and to others it may look like a fool's errand, do it anyway. If nothing else do it to know that you did it. I may never sell a million copies of this book or go on to change people's lives, but I know that I did not quit when I had every reason to. I did not give up even when everything told me I wanted to. And win or lose, no one can ever take away the, "I did it," factor. And that is worth a thousand don't do its.

Most important are God and family. Yes, I know it sounds hypocritical, but it is only after facing your demons that you understand why they came into your life and what your role was in attracting them. You see, the thing they do not tell you in Bible school is that the universe and God will test your resolve. They send people and situations into your life not to harm you but to teach you either something about humanity or something about yourself. My problem was I spent so long looking at my tiny egotistical view of things. I saw that my mom died, my dad died, I was abandoned, I was molested. What I did *not* see was why. And that is the biggest question of all, I think. Why do we have to go through things? Why do we have to hurt and suffer? And the closest I have been able to work out is to use the experience to help others.

Émilie du Châtelet first proposed the law of conservation of energy. It is more commonly understood to be, "that energy can neither be created nor destroyed; rather, it can only be transformed or transferred from one form to another." For example, a person is having a great day. The customer goes into the coffee shop, and there is no line. The individual's favorite pastry is in stock, and he or she is radiating positivity. The customer then interacts with the cashier. Now whatever kind of day the cashier is having, he or she will be left in a more positive mood than when the customer first entered. Why? Because the positive person transferred some of his or her good mood and goodwill to the cashier. Whether it was the customer smiling at the cashier, saying a few kind words, or feeling generous and left a tip. Whatever it was, it is a fundamental law of thermodynamics that positive energy will spread.

Conversely, negative energy will spread in the same way. It is up to you to decide what kind of force you want to give to the world. Will you make it better or worse? Will you choose to use your negative experiences or setbacks to help someone else or hinder them. Just as positive people uplift, hurt people hurt. And that has nothing to do with God. We are born with free will and the ability to decide every day, every minute what we will do with our lives. God, like any good parent, loves us and wants the best for us. But also like any good parent, we as children must fall so that we can learn how to pick ourselves back up. We must be abandoned so we learn how to survive and thrive on our own.

And again, it might seem ironic that I lean on family when, after all this, family has been the least stable comfort I have been afforded. Family is not just blood; it is the people you choose to make brothers and sisters. I have amazing people who have stood by me when I did not even want to be around myself anymore. And they still encouraged me not to give up. They still loved me past the pain. And they often saw the version of me I could not see myself because I did not think she existed. But the people who love you will acknowledge the faults you possess. And they will always remind you that faults are not what make you. It is the pureness of your heart, the integrity of your convictions, and the strength of you character that will make you who you are. It falls to each person to reveal that side, which often is the most daunting task of all, to truly let people see the fractured person underneath. But the beautiful thing about that is once you let them see you, it frees you to see your true self and what you can be.

The final lesson I learned is to love myself. And to give myself a break. To focus on the good and work on the bad, knowing that every day is an opportunity to make it better than the day prior because you know if you keep moving, you will get there. No matter what may come. Love yourself, love others. We are all in this together, and together we will survive.

Afterword

I've never been a fan of roller coasters. While the rush is amazing, it's also terrifying. So after everything in life, to have seemingly found happiness, well to say the least, I was skeptical. I was far into my healing journey but still very unsure and insecure in my decision-making. I went by the doctrine of do no harm. In whatever decision I made, first came family and our well-being. Second came God and the universe.

One of the almost impossible tasks is to have faith. To base all your hope on external sources and to trust them to help you in sometimes desperate situations. As I wrote earlier, I like to call then hidden angels. These are the heroes who go about life genuinely making other people's lives better. They are the firefighters who rescue people from a burning building. They are the people who put themselves in harm's way to protect others, even if they are strangers. They are the brave individuals who have the courage to speak out for what is right and protect the unprotected. That's not to say it can't be as simple as feeding someone hungry. I think God shows up in the energy of positivity and the love of one human being for another.

Are miracles real? I have no idea. "Maybe" would be my best answer. In my belief, is God real? Absolutely, even if you may not choose to see it or acknowledge it. Much like a parent is always holding the light on for their children, so, too, I think is God. And once I had this tower moment, I knew that I had to do what I could to be worthy of it. Even if it was just being overly nice to someone who obviously was having a bad day. It gave me an immense satisfaction to see people happy after their interactions with me. Sort of like the domino effect. I figured through transference of energy, if I spread hope and positivity, it would have far-reaching effects. Then I saw how through this theory, if people decided to live conscious of spreading hope and positivity, we could change the world. Admittedly not the entire world, but enough to make a difference.

Printed in the United States
by Baker & Taylor Publisher Services